Tip it, Pat it

Written by Caroline Green

Illustrated by Ángeles Peinador

Collins

mat
. . .

sit

3

mat

sit

dip

6

tip

dip

tip

pat

pin

pat

pin

/t/

14

10

✿ Review: After reading ✿

Use your assessment from hearing the children read to choose any GPCs and words that need additional practice.

Read 1: Decoding

- Use grapheme cards to make any words you need to practise. Model reading those words, using teacher-led blending.
- Look at the "I spy sounds" pages (14–15) together. Ask the children to point out as many things as they can in the picture that begin with the /t/ sound. (*table, toadstools, teacher, tea, tree, tubs, tiger, tortoise, toucan, tomatoes, ten, teddy*)
- Ask the children to follow as you read the whole book, demonstrating fluency and prosody.

Read 2: Vocabulary

- Look back through the book and discuss the pictures. Encourage the children to talk about details that stand out for them. Use a dialogic talk model to expand on their ideas and recast them in full sentences as naturally as possible.
- Work together to expand vocabulary by naming objects in the pictures that children do not know.
- Ask the children to mime the following to check their understanding of the verbs:

    tip   **dip**   **pat**

Read 3: Comprehension

- Ask the children to describe a picture they have painted or made. What did they use?
- Look at the front cover and ask questions about the title, looking back at pages 7 and 10 if necessary:
    - What did the child tip on their picture? (e.g. *glitter*)
    - Why did the child pat the paper after they had put sequins on it? (e.g. *to make the sequins stick to the picture*)